Speechless

Finding My Voice Within My Struggles

Holly Grossenheider

BookLeaf
Publishing

India | USA | UK

Made with ❤ on the BookLeaf Publishing Platform

www.bookleafpub.in

www.bookleafpub.com

Dedication

To my family. This year has been hard, but we will make it. I love you all.

Preface

This poetry collection comes from a period of my life when I was subjected to turmoil from those around me, including those you are supposed to trust. Needless to say that this period affected my family in ways that caused much pain, and confusion among all of us. As a result, I turned to writing to help me cope with all the pain that I experienced, and continue to do so as of this writing. The poems I produced here are raw, channeled from my experiences and feelings as it was the only place I was not being shut down by others who refused to listen. As I have recently learned, poetry can be a good way to heal, and let your voice be expressed without fear or judgment. This is especially true when those who you would think would listen, just dismiss you. So without further ado, I will now let the poems speak for themselves.

Acknowledgements

There have been many people who have inspired me during the writing of this book. First, I want to thank my children, Khloe, Miley, and Sophia, all of whom this book wouldn't have been possible. I hope that by publishing this book, I've shown them that you are never too old to achieve a dream. Next, I would like to thank those who have caused chaos in my life in this past year. Without them, I would have never been inspired to put my thoughts and feelings of such a dark time to paper. I won't individually name names, as it would be a very long list, but these people know who they are and what they have done for my inspiration. Finally, a special thanks goes out to you, the reader, for coming into the depths of my mind and the hurt that I have experienced. Without you, this book wouldn't be possible. However, despite its dark tone of what I have written, I hope you enjoy them.

With many thanks,

Holly

1. Drowning

I am drowning,
My tears are around me.
My eyes they cannot see,
I am drowning amidst a summer's storm.

With eyes always watching me
As a shadow in the night creeps stealthily.
The cards are stacked against me,
With no clear direction
in which to go.

I am drowning,
Drowning, drowning,
My sorrows are all my own.
Someday, somehow, my sorrows will
lead me home.

2. Voices in my Head

Voices in my head,
I cannot go,
I cannot tread.

Thoughts and feelings
Keep me awake,
anxiety alone
I cannot shake.

Children sleeping soundly
In their dreams.
My heart is empty as
it seems.

The voices surround me
like a ghost
I'm missing someone,
I feel I am toast.

If the memories of the
Voices fail to drift away,
I do not know where I'll be
Tomorrow or today.

3. Holes

There's a hole inside me
That nobody can see.
Torment of the situation

That nobody can understand.
Chaos amidst the family
Which shall I choose?

No matter what,
I am bound to lose.
Fear often surrounds me,
Losing everything that I have.

Love is lost, lies are found
Will I be going into the ground?
These holes that are within me
Burn red hot like the
smoldering sun.

Searing into my skin,
pain into my soul
Waiting for me to
go out of control.

Losing everything I
 hold dear in a flash,
Waiting for the inevitable fall.

The holes that reside inside me
Will consume me to the end.
One thing I know for sure
These holes are becoming my only friend.

4. Lady

*Tan and Black
and white was she,
Gentle in demeanor.*

*She loved a car ride
and a treat,
and those who
would just see her.*

*Chasing critters
all day long
Was her life's
choice of song.*

*Lady was her name,
She captured our
Hearts and minds
With a paw print or two.*

*She loved to bark,
especially in the dark
when the whole world
was sleeping.*

The time came
 to say goodbye,
Black eyes,
labored breathing.

My soul ripped in two.
alone in the room
as the tears came.

Someday my Lady Bird,
I will be finding you.
Everything then will
be right as rain.

5. Family

Family is a virtue
Which not everyone understands
Blood can hurt you
Quicker than the sand.

Lies are spread quickly
From sea to shining sea,
Nobody seems to care
How this has affected me.

People say I'm crazy
That I'm not fit to be a mom
Slowly pushed aside
From the east as from the west.

All I can do is let you go,
Wish you the very best
We may be blood, yes this is true
After my experience of 2024
I no longer believe I can trust you.

Trust is easily broken
No one seems to care
The hurt and the pain,

Broken families and the shame
Never will be the same again

If there's one thing I've learned
This is my vow,
During the hard times,
I can only rely on me now.

6. Rising From the Ashes

Rising from the ashes
Like a phoenix from the sun,
Those who have tried to stop me
From telling my truth.

I keep on saying what I believe
To everyone's dismay
I keep on going and going
To work and home everyday.

I'm done with the liars
I'm done with the manipulation
I've had enough of the abuse.

No longer will I be nice,
No longer will I be civil.
I am rising from the ashes
A phoenix forever I will be.

7. Corruption

Corruption is all around me
The place I call home,
The things I say and do,
I am not allowed to roam.

Corruption twists the words
like a knife,
Until it fits their own.
Lies often run rampant,
Unable to say what I feel and see.

Corruption calls me crazy,
I am not believed
What they're hoping for is
That I will be deceived.

Corruption has destroyed my family
It has taken all I've got,
I will not stay silent,
For this is my vow

Corruption will be defeated,
Sent back to yesteryear.
I will rise from the ashes,

I will be heard
This I make myself clear.

8. Neurodivergent

I am neurodivergent,
Clad with ADHD,
There is also Autism,
That has affected me.

I feel like I don't belong,
Within the club of normalcy.
I'm constantly told to smile,
I look like I faced a thousand deaths,

Socializing with others, it's so hard to do,
I can't read others cues,
Despite wanting to.
I forget my focus,
Bouncing from one thing to the next,

Masking is getting harder,
I didn't choose to be this way,
People don't understand.
This seems to be my lot,

I may have to stay away,
I don't gel well with the neurotypical,
I will never fit right in,

Yes, I am neurodivergent,
This is how I am.

9. Life Lessons

1. *Your voice often drowns amongst the crowd.*
2. *Real family isn't blood, they're often furry with 4-legs.*
3. *Attorneys hear the rustle of dollars before they hear your words.*
4. *Write like your soul depends on it.*
5. *Cats are like people, they can be good despite the rancid attitudes they put out.*
6. *Strength is necessary, you don't realize how much you have.*
7. *Trust the universe, it is massive and never-ending.*
8. *Mowing is a never-ending means for sneezing.*
9. *Choosing a paint color for a bathroom can signify new beginnings.*
10. *Just keep swimming, even when you're drowning.*

No matter what, I stand in the lesson, surviving because I am alive.

10. 2024…The Year That Never Ends

In my life completely, lies the year 2024,
The year that never ends, striving to dole out more.
Pain and suffering screaming within me, to which I
cannot see,
My soul within me is crushed to capacity.

It has pushed my sanity to the brink of hell and back,
Some days I feel completely sick,
I can't see where I'm going, spiraling down into a pit.

Criminal cases, divorce, and parental alienation laying
on so thick,
So many gloomy days come my way, I'm sure that this is
it.

In many ways, 2024 has made me feel left behind,
Like a hamster on a wheel, there's no direction in my
life.
My mind is never free, the chains of despair cut me
down like a knife,
Many times I have thought, "What have I done with my
life"?

Amidst the chaos in my mind, I am waiting for some
clarity.
I try to understand myself, try to get my head above
water,
However, this year has decided to continue to allow me
to falter.

Despite this glimmer of hope, 2024 still has more chaos
in mind for me,
The taste of death and despair are everywhere, to which I
take my bow.

I back away, don't want to stay in the hell that is my
world,
But the hell keeps on coming, as if I'm on a tilt-o-whirl.

I am praying that my neverending torture will soon
come to a head,
No doubt the stench of rotten lies continues to seep into
my soul

My thoughts and opinions don't matter, the law has told
me so
2024 sets out to destroy me, to which it has done,
At this point I'm tired, tired of my mind being on the
run.

It is now September, the chaos this year has brought will
still pursue
My soul and mind will remain in a stupor, not knowing
what to do.
Things will remain chaotic, I wish this year would end,
On and on it goes, 2024 you are not a friend.

11. A Poem For Three: The Bickering

I am a mother, struggling on my own
Fighting the battle cries, of my daughters
As we travel home.
I am exhausted, hearing her yell
her battle cry, at her sister,
demanding that she listen.

Mother hen of the year, that is what you are.
Flapping your gums, both near and far,
I can't get a word in, my voice is drowned out,
The bickering commences, and it doesn't stop.
Like a toddler banging on pots and pans
My head is throbbing.

I am the oldest, I tell you what to do
Little sister, until the day is through.
You listen to me, nothing else matters
You don't even listen to Mom,
You make her nerves shatter.

You throw your tantrums,
Always get your way,
Mom likes you better,

I wish you'd go away.

I am the youngest, the smallest of them all,
Two older sisters, who always take the fall.
I don't mean to not listen,
I can't always understand.
I am autistic, which I don't always see,
Like a tornado in a storm, my emotions sometimes take
over me,
It is you dear sister, who doesn't understand.

You always boss me around, don't give me time
To process directions that flow in my mind,
You too, overwhelm Mom with
Flapping your gums,
Complaining, and whining
About everything under the sun.

Oh, dear girls, I've heard enough
Bickering and fighting,
Please don't get rough.
How about we be silent as the breeze,
 And be still as a chair?

We are almost home, and will soon be there.
We are almost out of this car,
Please get away from each other,

Both go far and don't get in between,
You both drive me crazy,
I wish you could see what I mean.

12. Dear Me

The year is 2024, and you have gone through hell,
People have talked you down,
Made you feel crazy,
Feeling only 1-inch tall.
Please always remember,
That is not the truth at all.

People are huge assholes,
Most of them don't give a shit.
They only want to believe the worst in people,
Without throwing a fit.

These people don't care
How their words tear
Deep into a person's soul,
Stabbing it with a knife,
Leaving it destroyed.

For you, it's been like a whirlwind,
Like being stuck in the eye of a hurricane,
Not knowing who to trust,
And whether things will ever be the same.

Although this year is not yet over,

Like David and Goliath,
You have much still to endure.
Please be proud of how far you've come,
With this, not everyone is able.

In the meantime,
Please be kind to yourself.
You are like a phoenix,
Rising from the ashes,
One who cannot be shattered.

Those who have wronged you,
Will eventually meet their fate.
Karma is a bitch,
But you will have to wait.

Dear me,
It is five years later,
The year is 2029.
Your oldest has graduated,
And another is due next year.

You are now successful
In every area of life,
While those who hurt you
Are being stabbed with their

Hurtful knives.

Just remember, don't ever forget,
The difficulties of 2024,
You will always be you,
And your thoughts and opinions
Are worth so much more.

13. When This Hell is Over

When this hell is over,
There are so many things I'd like to do,
The first thing I plan on doing,
is coming straight to you.

We will hold each other
With all our might and our strength,
Never to be separated, never to part,
When that day comes,
I will hold you in my heart.

14. Time Heals All Wounds

They say that time heals all wounds,
But I don't think that's true.

For all the good times that we had,
I can't help but missing you.

Children grow up and move on,
Leaving me here alone.

I can't help wondering how you've faired
Or whether you still care.

No matter the distance
Or what other people say,

You will always be in my heart,
Forever you will stay.

15. My Inner Thoughts

Things in my head that no one knows,
Thoughts of loss that torment me,
Anxiety has consumed me,
I feel as if it will never stop.

Depression has consumed me
Like a tidal wave, about to drown me.
I'm not sure whether to turn left or right,
What I say doesn't matter or how I feel.

Guilt is imminent,
With no chance to defend.
People keep on coming,
I fear it will never end.

No matter what this life brings me,
What I've learned is this,
No matter who you are
And where you come from,
You are always on someone's list.

16. Never Again

Never again will I trust,
 People in this world.
They treat you the same
 As trash in a dumpster.

Never again, will I be able to feel,
A sense of love and acceptance.
Oh wait, I never had it in the first place.
Some say I'm too much to handle.

Never again, will I try to find
my sense of belonging.
My purpose, my inner circle.
I was born as a lone wolf,
Not meant for traveling in packs.

Never again, will I try to rise up
and do the right thing.
Shit comes my way,
People mock me
As if I'm the latest circus display.

As my tolerance wanes,
I come to this conclusion,

I'll be fine on my own,
But don't ever again
Come my way.

17. The Anger That Dwells Within Me

The anger that dwells within me,
Bubbling up inside,
Waiting for the rush of release
Like a gush of water from the tide.

The anger is coming,
Like a lion's roar.
Nobody seems to understand
What I'm yelling for.

Many people have suppressed me,
Keeping me silent.
Time marches on,
I'm now faced alone against a giant.

Unable to express myself,
Raises the anger trapped inside,
Unable to be released,
With nowhere to go.

If I let this anger out,
People will deem me crazy,
Question my intentions,

And my abilities.

All I wanted was to be heard,
Be treated the same,
Instead, I am stuck with anger,
Forever it will stay.

18. Northern Lights

Oh, to see the Northern Lights,
Where do I begin?
It's beauty is incomparable
To the very rarest gem.

Its reds and pink swirl across the sky,
As if it were Valentine's Day.
The auras that flash about,
I wish they could stay.

If I were to see the Lights again,
I will wait to see,
The purples and blues
Swirling around as if they were royalty.

I hope the Lights come back again,
I can't wait to see
Its beauty and wonder all around,
Especially when it is surrounding me.

19. The Silence

I am silent
So I am told,
Or my family
Will unfold.

I can't say what's
on my mind,
the truth is
mine to find.

If I find the truth,
it is mine,
but must stay silent
at all times.

If I speak, I am told
my thoughts are too bold.
I am crazy,
the truth comes out,

Staying silent,
kills me
In the midst of chaos
there's no doubt.

20. Still Standing

I'm still standing.
I'm still here,
to the dismay of others
who wish I'd disappear.

I've survived,
bent and broken,
While those around me,
cackle like a witch in the night.

Many have cursed me,
So have I,
among those in this
kangaroo court.

It's not over,
don't count me out,
I'm still standing,
That's what I'm all about.

21. Narcissists

Narcissists will hurt you,
often make you cry.
Narcissists will make
you question yourself
to the brink of hell and back
and you won't understand why.

Narcissists will turn people
against you, til nobody
has your back.
Narcissists will take
everything you've got
then you take the blame.

After all, that is the name
of their game.
Lord help you if you get mad,
the narcissist will pull out
the "crazy" card,
life for you will never
remain the same.

One thing that I learned of
in my experience

with a narcissist,
keep your eyes open
and mouths shut
or you may find yourself
in the deepest darkest pit.

www.ingramcontent.com/pod-product-compliance
Lightning Source LLC
LaVergne TN
LVHW010924200726
843509LV00013B/2049